NAMIBIA

Namibia, known as the land of the brave, is a stunning country in southwest Africa. Explore its sandy dunes and grassy plains and discover the wonders it has to offer through pictures accompanied by haiku and/or cinquain poetry.

Charles R Haffner

CINQUAIN

Alta H Haffner

HAIKU

N A M I B I A

WE DEDICATE THIS BOOK TO JADEN RETIEF.

Most of the images are credited to Jaden, He took these on his vacation to Namibia at the end of 2020.

© **2022 Charles R Haffner**

© **2022 Alta H Haffner**

First Edition: 979-8439902170
2024 Second Edition: 978-0796174413

ALL RIGHTS RESERVED

Barren
desert tree rests
from the beaming sun rays.
Looks so out of place and thirsty
today.

Searching
for a bathtub,
but it was too damn hot.
Lazy elephant cools off in
puddles.

**cool water splashing
lush green soon to be a treat
fun in heat of day**

Staring
ahead, tired
from all of the moving.
Pointy head bison wants to rest
again.

rambunctious when raged
old superbly powerful
respected giant

Laughing
hyena twins
not from the jokes, but the
silly camera man taking
pictures.

mischievous grinning
prowling for a tasty feast
partners in this crime

Sweaty
boar runs away
from working on this hot
summer day, not caring about
money.

even in the heat
camouflaged and running slow
still peaceful retreat

Spotted
neckers cuddle
under a blue sky as
the clouds overhead pillow them
kisses.

**cutest lovers kiss
almost touching fluffy clouds
no wedding bells yet**

Waiting,
relaxed as time
sits still this bird thrilled
since only a camera not
poachers.

pose for the perfect
the lens of a kind human
no danger this time

Chilling,
flexing at the
jealous giraffe that looks
at this gorgeous hill wishing he's
taller.

all stretched out sneaking
lizard baking in the sun
new strange acquaintance

Awkward
moment today,
as we are staring blankly
at two midgets taking pictures
of us.

beauty of nature
wonder if we get a treat
maybe next time 'round

I first
was so thirsty,
but now I'm so hungry.
My appetite is teased by small
morsels.

he wanted a friend
his tummy had other plans
now both lost a friend

I do
wonder if their
eyesight is worse than my
thinking that I'm so completely
concealed.

Pride
sometimes is not
as important as
just being plain lazy. Who cares
really?

resting a little
your beauty is a trophy
to those with no soul

Sour face
waiting today
lying by the tall grass,
so tired from yawning yesterday.
Bored cat.

grumpy lazy yawn
awaiting his queen at lunch
fiesta for two

Out in
the desert a
tree is sharing its green.
Many shaded thriving leaves, not
money.

**view to be admired
a once in a lifetime glimpse
Namibia's gift**

Walking
so casually
away with all the time
in the world, bird that's pleasantly
baking.

Watching
her watching us.
Dust clouds in the desert,
testing out the horns hoping it
protects.

**opposites attract
a waterhole gathering
a happy ending**

Drinking
herd cautiously
slurps water in such gulps
moving on to another type
of place.

spot the odd one out
it is difficult to see
only see beauty

Black and
white Life's never
This simple, animals
Sharing the plains under the still
Hot sun

brown spotted or striped
black and white all the same now
need to quench a thirst

Quad drinks.
Still air desert,
trying to survive, since
nature's beauty brings danger to
unfit.

Battles
To stay on top
Alpha won't give up his
respected spot being leader
of pack .

look at these humans
writing about us from far
we should charge dollars

Ostrich
drinking with some
others, some wading while
others take a cool sip of this
water.

did you spot the crow
he took his fair chance quickly
giants not bothered, yet

Black and
white stripes drinking
water so dangerously.
Camouflage is not smart, but is
required.

**different angles
they are watching from all sides
in case of danger**

Such green
sitting alone.
Beautiful tree welcomes
or is it mind games. Treachery
to some.

Lonely
tree sits quiet
as clouds appear on the
horizon bringing possibly
some rain.

Shyly
standing, afraid
of sticking out this day.
No green to show off, just a brown
decay.

Standing
tall, not afraid.
Striped tail is dragging on
the ground,while peering ahead not
caring.

**graceful elegance
take a stance for confidence
bow your head at dusk**

Resting.
Pride watches the field.
As the sun beams, grueling.
Another normal desert day
waiting.

warm thoughts
Are in his mind
Eyes bulging from his head
Lazy lion looks like he hates
Sweating .

**king of the jungle
even in the dry desert
hunt and nap**

Looking
But not playing
Only caring about the
Awful Heat on this Sunny and
Slow day

Panting,
never happy.
Watching food run away.
Catching her breath, beaming sun pounds
away.

Dying
grass all around.
Catching a breather now.
Praying for some camouflage quick
right now.

Crossing,
yet wondering
how this got here right now.
Roadway in the desert, my heart is
thumping.

crossing all boundaries
in the Sahara desert
dusty sandy roads

Wrinkly
ancient thing stands.
Like an old man waiting
for his bus to come, his horn does
not honk.

Living
colors stand out,
like flowers in barren
fields in the middle of deadly
winter.

**your brightest crimson
a survival instinct now
desert and insects**

Perked up,
ears listening
for some good news, but
only hears the sun beating down
today.

the savannah's fox
crouches as it stalks some prey
fluffy tail alert

Figures
climbing such dunes.
Sandy hills to play in
or desert graveyard to bury
you in?

the heat of the day
the midday thirst and sun glow
wait the sunset hour

Fingers
poking through sand.
Out of the grave, coming
to seek a new land to drink some
water.

Painting.
I wish was mine.
Drawn to my hungry mind.
Beautiful place I'm wishing to
die in.

Sunset
after such noons
Refreshing our moods from
The African desert scorching
hot days

**naturally fall
rocks balancing all beauty
in awe with nature**

**sunset horizon
shady amber and chocolate
still as hot as noon**

Mother
and the father
Scolding their kid , playing
in the bathtub too long again
Parents

untamed and sky high
old soul, forgotten tales
protecting your young

**rock shelter and caves
"white lady" art protected
heritage site now**

This dates back to over 2000 years ago

remind me again
a glorious sunset glow
memories linger

Chewing
of flesh off the
Bones as these two leopards
eat during their lazy after
Noon lunch

**a dry desert sun
awaiting the feast at noon
soon a siesta**

desert art, oh joy
simple and yet beautiful
sand and stones connect

Orange hills
sandy passage
Across the still desert
some trees at the bottom for some
Pictures

dusty road to walk
to the top of the mountain
no danger in sight

**colors of autumn
a hot sunny afternoon
no sudden showers**

cooling and quenching thirsty lionesses wait for a turn to slurp

Some say
Courage, I say
crazy for some trees to
Live in the middle of stupid
Desert

**amber and azure
a lonely walk of freedom
but worth the dawns view**

dunes at dawns greeting
a new found blessing start now
a thirst for love rise

landscape of dune peaks
sun greets early morning glow
picture perfect view

**fine art in desert
for tourist to admire
preserved in the sand**

**tired lazy seals
cool in the heat of the day
some catching a snooze**

a perfect morning
start hiking up the mountain
remember water

colorful textures
a glorious desert day
hyenas awake

**slow journey begins
an old man and a donkey
just another day**

**chameleon rests
not changing to light green soon
hues of desert sand**

**a rare victory
elephant got the best snack
hurrying to feast**

you beg for little
only sun and a fresh breeze
ancient quiver spear

engine stopped running
many seasons of weather
desert ornament

dunes stretched far and wide
always peaking exhaustion
seeking shade, not found

golden fragile twigs
shadows fall in afternoon
cotton clouds backdrop

an ancient vehicle
colors blending with desert
perfectly captured

ancient history
witness the beauty of this
the rocks holds secrets

camo
fail, as black and
white asses are hiding
in an ocean of green. Lions
see lunch

**orange windy road
a tree happily nourished
endless sahara**

ocean waves splashing
cooling the hot rocks today
azure clouds above

**travelling Namibia
exploring and reconnect
with your inner core**

About the Authors

Alta H Haffner   Charles R Haffner

Charles R Haffner

Charles R Haffner Was born in Baltimore Maryland and lived in Central Florida for 15 years. For the past two years, he has written several Books consisting of micro poetry.

He resides in South Africa with his wife and fellow Poet, Alta.

Alta H Haffner

Alta H. Haffner is a Haiku poet whose work captures the essence of precious, fleeting moments with simplicity and depth. Born with a deep appreciation for the beauty of brevity, Alta's Haiku poems reflect her keen observation of nature and her ability to evoke emotions in just a few short lines.

Drawing inspiration from the ever-changing seasons, the delicate balance of the natural world, and the quiet whispers of every new dawn, Alta's Haiku poems invite readers to slow down, pause, and appreciate the present moment. With a handful of syllables, she allows her readers to contemplate.

Through her Haiku poetry, Alta H. Haffner reminds us of the beauty that can be found in simplicity, the power of mindfulness, and the importance of being fully present in each moment.

www.ingramcontent.com/pod-product-compliance
Lightning Source LLC
Chambersburg PA
CBHW042349300426
44109CB00034B/24